TO THE
MONSTERS
OF MY PAST

TO THE
MONSTERS
OF MY PAST

CAMERON CREWS

Library of Congress Control Number: 2020916617
ISBN: Hardcover   978-1-6641-2843-9
                  Softcover   978-1-6641-2842-2
                  eBook   978-1-6641-2841-5

Illustrated by Cassie Legg

Print information available on the last page.

Rev. date: 11/12/2020

To order additional copies of this book, contact:
Xlibris
844-714-8691
www.Xlibris.com
Orders@Xlibris.com
814981

CONTENTS

DEDICATIONS

To Ken Crews, Patti Crews, Carter Crews Korte, and Kelly Crews Dayton, for the unwavering love and support they have shown me since the day I was born. I'm so lucky you're mine.

To Julian Alderson, Sophie Pearlstein, Morgan Griffith, Georgia Henley, and Courtney Vrij, for being by my side through the best and the worst of it. Thank you for being my chosen family.

To Cassie Legg, for her loyal friendship and creative inspiration. Thank you for taking the time to beautifully illustrate this book.

To everyone who thinks I'm writing about them. You're probably right.

And to Ike Crews, always.

Illustrations By Cassie Legg

TO THE MONSTERS OF MY PAST

To the monsters of my past—
I bid you a bittersweet farewell.
I've finally escaped your tower,
Slayed the dragon, broke the spell.

And although those dark days
Made me appreciate the bright,
I leave those harsh memories behind
With every line that I write.

And here is my diary …

WARNING

Before you go reading ahead
I must warn you of what comes next

There's pain in these pages
They're full of despair
You'll relive my heartbreaks
You may get nightmares

This isn't a happy book in verse
To get to the happiness, hardship comes first
I write of failures, monsters, miscrowned princes
I bring up those emotions often kept at a distance

This isn't for the fainthearted
This book is written for the brave
But by facing the battles head-on
I hope you feel saved.

ELMER'S

Mom's hosting an event
Dad's working overseas
Carter's at cheer practice
Ike's with me

My parents leave me be
My sister's got an ego
But Ike, my big brother,
Is my favorite superhero

We all drift apart
For life or by choice
But Ike pulls us back in
Like some magic, loving force

Why should I be better?
I'll always have you
Our family goes array
But Ike is the glue

PRINCESS IN PRISON

He always wore a suit
Her shoes would match her purse
They had everything they needed
But their blessings were their curse

They lived in a big house
Healthy dogs, cats, and children
The hedge kept them safely in
But money couldn't fence their villains

They had so much material stuff
Their life was full of privilege
But when the party lights came on
They stood without a village

She saw herself a queen
Her social scene, her court
But as hard times came her way
She had no true support

He saw himself an honest man
He worked hard and built his life
But he grew more and more dissatisfied
He felt disconnected from his wife

He couldn't understand her emotions
She was broken by the death of her rock
The demons silently crept in
Though the castle doors were locked

He found relief through drinking
Suddenly tainted by success
The more he drank in private
The more she grew depressed

Their demons became constant
They pushed his hand to the glass
Hers kept her in bed for days
All alone except her cat

At a time, their life was perfect
Then crept in their villains
The castle they built and loved
Became their own personal prison

VACANT

It was a bang in the night
The silence's swift abruption
A small child waking in cold fright
To the evening's mysterious disruption

Decisively out of bed
She took her bear up in her arms
Not knowing what she'd find
Not expecting her mother could be harmed

But the bang in the night
Was more than a simple creak
Something was wrong with her father
Her mother on the floor, fragile and weak

Dad's face was numb
All she could see was black and red
She wasn't sure where the blood came from
Until she noticed her mom's head

"Am I bleeding?" Mom yelled
Dad turned away with an empty glare
The man they knew and loved, there physically
But his character no longer there

NOT MY FAIRYTALE

She once lived in a joyous castle
Happy parents, loud siblings present
But she blinked and lost her tiara
The prosperous reign came and went

A single princess was left in the decrepit castle
With the venomous king and weak queen
New devils replaced her siblings
Named vodka, xanax, nicotine

She had only known goodness
What's happening? She was confused
She'd call and pester her siblings
"Are you coming home anytime soon?"

She knew her parents were in trouble
They weren't OK, she could see
But she was still so young and dependent
"Mom and Dad, what about me?"

The royals stopped joining daily life
What day was it? It's October?
Who would drive the carriage to school
When neither parent was sober?

They were in the same bodies
God, she loved them with her whole heart
But her parents weren't the same people
She watched as her fairytale lifestyle
Slowly fell apart

TO STAY OR TO GO

We packed our bags full
Of memories
Of optimism
Hoping he'd agree with the doctors
An intervention of love
Underlined with criticism

We didn't want to leave
But Mom said
We would have no choice
She was scared as well
Firm but shaken
In her tone of voice

So we packed our suitcases full
Then left to await the news
Would Dad agree to go to rehab?
Where would we go if he refused?

GHOST

I'd hear her in the pantry
Stocking up for hibernation
I'd hear her movements in her bedroom
Avoiding disappointment and confrontation

The days were her nights
And in the evenings, she haunted
Wearing her bathrobe of white
Feeling lonely and unwanted

She had become a ghost
Plaguing her loved ones nearby
You wouldn't even know she was there
If it weren't for the rustles
And the subdued cries

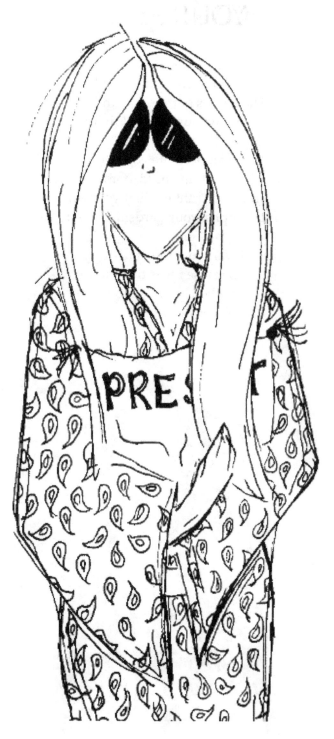

YOUR STORY

I want to write your story
But it isn't mine to tell
The details both brutal and gory
How did we survive that living hell?

I want to write your story
Chaos out of my mind, onto the page
But you want to tell it yourself
Your triumphs, your hardships, your stage

I want to write your story
Because I was there too
But when I put pen to paper
The protagonist is you

I'M SORRY

For years, to me,
You were a defender
Piecing me back together
When I was broken
Our days together
Marked by true love and splendor
But now
All that's left
Are words unspoken.

I never thought
There'd come a day
When our lives
Would grow apart
And although you wanted
Me to stay
I broke from you
And broke your heart.

I know you think
I just disappeared
Creating pain
Without a cure
One thing I wish
From me
You'd hear
It broke my heart to break yours.

UNNECESSARY NECESSITY

He was everything she thought she wanted,
But their love was everything it shouldn't be.
It was destructive.
It was erratic.
It was necessary.

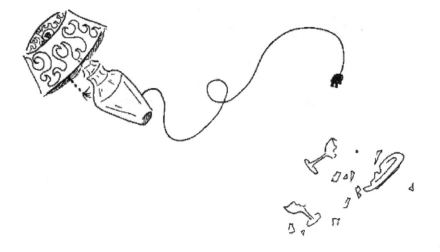

6325

A happy couple in the late '90s
Found the dream house
Where their flourishing family belonged.

A red-brick Tudor
With beveled windows,
Like in the wife's dreams,
Created happiness
The couple's purchase prolonged.

This family had aberrant purposes in mind
For what most saw
As a welcoming room with marble floor.

Many experiments and tournaments
Led the kids to find
Rollerblading, skateboarding, and soccer games
Proved much more fun indoors.

The kitchen,
More than a place for cooking,
Hosted feasts for people of all sorts.

Such as school-colored pancakes on Fridays,
A tradition the mother still strongly exhorts.

Past the library and through the back door,
You'd enter the jungle
Serving as a playground
For adolescents and pets.

Neighborhood kids all met here to rumble,
Playing all games from laser tag to space cadets.

The house's walls witnessed all,
From convivial times to heated diatribes,
And firsthand saw the family drift apart.

A house once filled with ubiquitous love and joy
Over time became defunct,
And in succession did the tenants depart.

Now in the house remains only two—
The mother and the juvenile.
At all different times did the others leave
For ambitions, maturity, or exile.

A fair share of sadness existed within the walls,
But for all the bad,
There remained just as much good.

The foundation provided strong support
Physically and emotionally,
As any memorable childhood house should.

The children grew up as they all do,
And across the world they did roam.

But no matter how great
Their new abodes prove,
No other place will truly be home.

WRECKING BALL

First, they fenced it in
Placing my home within a cage
I felt trapped by emotion myself
Filled with sadness, agony, rage

Then it was completely disconnected
Put to sleep by shutting it off the grid
All the life had been sucked out
The historic deed had been outbid

Finally, they demolished my home
Unaware of the pain they were causing
The foundation ripped apart
Without remorse, without even pausing

They destroyed the sports court, the playhouse, the garden
Tearing the house and my childhood apart
When they took the wrecking ball to my room
I felt the impact in my heart

DO I HOLD A PLACE
IN YOUR HEART?

I know our love had truth
The deep emotion, the passion I felt
But now I fear the memory of me
Is no more than a notch in your belt

PUZZLING

I thought we would last forever
I believed my one true love was you
We fit together like puzzle pieces
But now I puzzle with someone new ...

Isn't that puzzling?

LIARS

We swore our distance
Proved no fault,
But in that phrase,
We lied.

You assured me
I would always
Know my worth,
But in that vow,
You lied.

I pledged
To not
Push you away,
But I, too,
Eventually lied.

I let my heart
Slowly break
Instead of
Simply trying.

Nothing left but
Pride to blame
For our flame
Slowly dying.

The roots of our love
Ripped from my heart,
We couldn't stop the lying.

GO, GIRL

What are you doing, stupid girl?
He doesn't love you like he said
What are you doing, stupid girl?
You're not the one in his bed

Why are you crying, lonely girl?
His love is less than you deserve
Why are you crying, lonely girl?
Some self-respect, you should conserve

If he really was the one for you
He'd own up and truly show it
But he's left you feeling alone and lost
His love proven counterfeit

So wipe your tears,
Maybe smoke a joint,
You're too good for him
And that's the point.

This is just a step
Toward a love that's true
And before you find
The perfect match
You must fall back
In love
With you

Go and prove you're not a stupid, lonely girl.

FIGHT ALL NIGHT

I reach out and reply
To see how you're doing
No matter what
I always hope you're all right
But now our conversations
So quickly turn dark
Simple words become venomous fights

You used to be
A light in my life
Then the candle burned out
And you're out of sight
And though we keep trying
This flame won't ignite

At one time
We felt
So soothingly right
But now
All we do is
Fight all night

UNCHANGEABLE TIMETABLE

Like a train on schedule pulling out of a station
I'll leave without fear or resignation
Although your love will always prove a temptation ...

I'll depart on time.

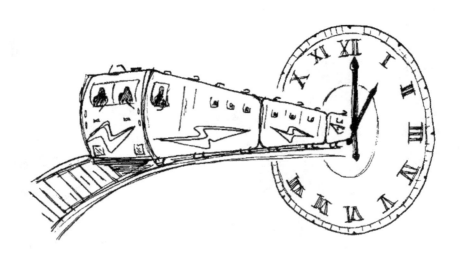

THE ANSWER'S IN
THE QUESTION

Do I really love you?
I often wonder
Or am I too scared to let go
Do I need another?

I know my feelings
At a time were true
But I'm no longer sure
That the one for me is you …

And the question is answered.

BE GONE

I wish I could chase out the sadness
Scare it right out of your brain
But you won't let me in, and it won't get out
Why do our own minds drive us insane?

I wish I could make you happy again
Without you around, it's just not the same
When you are here, you are not yourself
Your new composure radiates pain

I wish I could do more than watch.

THE ACCIDENT

He was a bully in her mind
Telling her she was a waste
She'd put these dark days behind
Planning the defeat, her heart raced

They'd been together for years
But at the expense of the host
With him around, it appeared
She was simply surviving at most

Sick of his constant harassment
And separation from those she cherished
She decided to shoot the irritant
He was evil; he must perish

Clouded by anger, sadness, depression
She took the gun up from the shelf
But when she killed that evil man
She also killed herself.

WE COULD FEEL HER

We could feel her in the room where she did it
Her family and cat refusing to leave
It was the last spot she'd been alive
Proving a reasonable place to grieve

We could smell the cleaner's bleach
Which left not a drop of blood on the floor
This new smell a poignant reminder
Grace wasn't with us anymore

We could see her, living and dead
As family movies played above the coffin of pink
Such harsh contrast of life and death
But we couldn't look away; we couldn't blink

We could hear her in the stories
That the family told to the funeral crowd
Grace's words of sarcasm and spunk
To even know her, we were proud

We could taste our very sorrow
Recognized by the salty flavor of tears
How could someone so young do this?
They only got her for 16 years

We could sense this living person
But that life had come and gone
How could this happen to one of us?
How could we ever try and move on

When we could sense her all around us.

GONE BY MORNING

We buried their baby
Only a couple days before
Nothing worse could happen to this family
Of that, we thought we were sure

But like most things we assumed
We were proven horribly, horribly wrong
Life had other plans for this family
We had no choice but to be strong

Just the night before
He was there, so loud and alive
Lighting up the room with his smile and humor
How could this great man ever die?

"I'll see you soon," we said
"End of the semester, won't be long"
When we said goodbye, he was there
But by the morning, he was gone

ANGEL LOVE

Sometimes in life
We lose the ones we love
They leave this world behind
To go somewhere above

Depart from their bodies
Painfully before goodbye
They leave this life behind
To go home to the sky

They close their eyes on earth
Their human life comes to an end
But they open them in heaven
With angel wings and angel friends

Even though they're gone from us
There's a piece of them at heart
Always carried with us
Although we're now apart

Don't sob too many tears
Even though it sure does help to cry
Trust in God and he'll restore you
Because angels can fly!

And since they can fly
They're constantly around
Eternally watching over us
Left here on the ground

It is hard to understand
That distant heaven is a better place
But there they're more than mortal humans
They're our personal angels of grace

When you feel cool wind
Or the warm sunshine
That's our angels letting us know
They're safe, happy, missing you

All among the divine.

EVENTUALLY

Eventually, you'll realize
Some questions will never be answered
And the future you've envisioned
Proved completely backward

The person you thought
You'd be with forever
Cannot be bothered
To make a single effort

You'll grow in time
And eventually show
You can get through anything
Much more than you know

By loving yourself
You'll come to see
This is the way
Things were meant to be

Eventually.

MISCHIEF MANAGED

Mischievous monsters in my head
Trying to tell me you're worth my time

But I know better

For now.

VICTORIA'S SECRET

Cameron told Sophia
Who swore she wouldn't ever tell
But Sophia accidentally told Charlie
"It just slipped out! Oh well!"

Charlie kept the secret
But Nico heard it through the phone
Which would have been fine
Had Nico been alone

But Nico was with Duncan
Whose always had a big mouth
(Must be 'cause he's from Texas
They talk a lot there down south)

Duncan mentioned it to some friends
Who told their friends, but only a few!
And within a couple hours
Practically the entire college town knew

Victoria originally told Cameron
Cameron should've kept her big mouth closed
But she went and blabbed the gossip
Victoria's secret now exposed!

The problem with telling one person
Each web of friends proves so complex
That now everybody in town knows
Victoria's never had sex!

PUT ME IN, COACH

I want all you have to offer
Much more than you've given me yet
Why don't we swallow our pride, get together?
On you, I'm willing to bet

Are you afraid to fully love me?
Do you still long for someone of the past?
Can't say I don't think of others too
But you're the one I want to last

I want you to be mine
Though I'm still afraid to fall
I dread getting hurt by you too
But trust me
I want it all.

HOURGLASS

I do not necessarily understand
Where all of life's time goes
When did I become this person?
When did lovers and friends turn into strangers? Foes?

When did I grow up?
Both on the outside and within
Why do people I love disappear?
Do I even ask what could have been?

I guess all that we can do
Is make the most of what is left
Because you can't rewind, redo
Time lost is gone—inevitable theft

TOO DAMN LONELY

I once again find that I'm not your only
Wish I wasn't so damn lonely
Wish I could grasp that you're just a phony
But it seems to me I'm too damn lonely
To actually let you go.

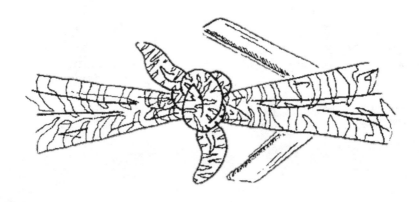

CHAPTER CONCLUDED

"I love you still
Like I loved you then"
You'll laugh and swear
She was just a friend
It's time to bring
This all to an end
We'll both move on
Hearts always mend
I'm finished now
Trying to play pretend
It's past time to bring
This all to an end.

TAKES DRINK

It was hard when I still thought
You were actually a good guy
But I know better now
You're fucking full of LIES.

HMM

Alas, our chapter ended
Our mess of emotion came to an end
We're on divergent paths now
Too much history to be friends

Once lost, scared, dependent
Looking to the past, I'm sure I've grown
Empowered, strong, independent
I'm happy on my own

Although something still seems missing
Perhaps I'm just drama-prone
But if moving on is what I wanted
Why do I still feel so alone?

MESSAGES I COULDN'T SEND

I miss you.
I miss running my hands through your thick brown hair.
I miss the funny circular shapes of your fingers and the way mine fit perfectly between them …
I miss the way you made me feel small and protected simply by holding me in your arms.

Do you miss me ever?
And I mean *really* miss me.
Do you miss me the way I miss you?
Do you miss me so deeply that it pains you to think I'm so far away?

Have you moved on?
Have you found someone to love the way you loved me?
I'm trying to move on, and to be honest, I want to.
We are too emotionally alike to find stability in the chaotic mess of our companionship.

You deserve better, and I won't blame you for letting me go.

TURNING THE PAGE

In order to move on
And to truly LIVE
You must open your heart
Swallow your pride
And forgive.

TOGETHER WE'RE NEW

I'm a little broken
You're a little messed up too
We put our halves together
And made a whole
Something new
A whole functioning person
Now made out of two
Who knew the recipe to happiness
Was simply me and you

BABUSHKA DOLL

You love the exterior
What you think is inside
But you don't know my demons
The defining troubles I hide

There's much more to me
Than what I present to the world
A few layers down, I'm a bit broken
A lost and damaged little girl

You don't know what haunts me
The small facts that make me whole
Is it even really <u>love</u>
If you love my shell and not my soul?

GO! GO! GO!

Your comfort zone is found at home—
the faces, places, spaces
you've grown up to know.
While your home will always be home,
some of the best parts of life
exist outside that comfort zone.

Some people choose to never leave.
Some do rarely.
Some do with ease.
Staying at home you may appease,
but there's all sorts of things you'll never see.

Through these next few verses,
I hope to inspire
A curiosity for the world
You'll hopefully desire.

The world is a two-way street—
Round, not flat.
And thankfully for that,
if you leave,
you can always return back.

Stepping out into the world
With an open mind,
You'll gain knowledge,
Experiences,
And souvenirs of all kinds.

Your previous one-sided outlook
Will soon distort
As you adventure
To castles,
Grasslands,

Or sail boat–filled ports

You'll meet a variety of people
Who at first
Might seem strange,
But once you get to know them,
Your opinion will change.

Earth is enormous
and contains extraordinary aspects
that for now are unknown.
It's like a big playground
All for you to roam.

You may go tomorrow
or once you are grown,
but to truly experience the world
you must step outside your comfort zone
and leave home.

Y'ALL CRAZY

It's taken me some time,
But now I FINALLY have come to know.
No one in this life is sane.
EVERYONE IS A GODDAMN PSYCHO!

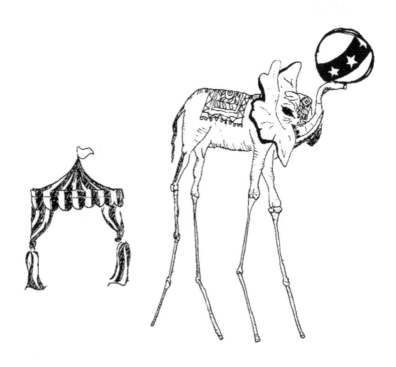

GOODBYE, NASTY MISS

The people who no longer serve you
No longer teach, please, excite, or care
Are not needed in your life
They've already contributed their share

Each person you cross has a purpose
Their stay either temporary or permanent
But the way they make you feel
Is their role's greatest determinant

Excuse the kind girl that's needy
Everyone needs love; that's no crime
Forgive the boy who's critical
He's just sad most of the time

But the one who has no purpose
Who you can easily dismiss
Is the one who's inconsiderate and mean
Just say goodbye to that nasty miss

You don't have to stay close
With everyone you've befriended
Let them go as lesson learned
Their guest appearance ended

But the ones who mean well in their intent
Deserve an everlasting part
For if they're truly a caring person
There's room for them in your heart.

CHOSEN FAMILY

Still stuck in Texas,
With no outside-world concern.
Failing the courses,
I was too stubborn to learn.
Still hung up on love
That called it quits and left.
Somewhere alone,
Feeling worthless and depressed.
Lost in this world,
Unable to forgive the past.
Questioning why self-made happiness
Just won't seem to last.
Watching life from above,
Physicality comes to an end.
These are the places I'd be
If it weren't for my friends.

JUST FRIENDS

Just friends
That's you and me
Nothing more, nothing here to see
I'm way too self sufficient to think of what could be
If there's more connection between us
I guess we'll wait and see

SCOTTISH STORM

A Scottish storm
I'm lying next to you
The clouds block the sun
The sky a navy-blue hue

We ignore our alarms
Day is canceled—rain
We take cover in the covers
The thunder we have to make

Too cold to leave the bed
Too lazy to put on clothes
Your window shaking ferociously
The Scottish wind blows

Midday, though it's still dark
My feelings for you keep growing
It's vocal, cold, intense
Storm shows no sign of slowing

A Scottish storm
I'm lying next to you
The rain's falling so hard
And I am too

TEMPORARY FAMILIARITY

Cardboard boxes
Single-use soap
Early-morning flights
Missing home

Where the hell will I live in a year?
I don't see my family enough, I fear

Worry for the future is always present
Life's clock ticking on my adolescence

I fear the impending unfamiliarity
Uncertainty glorifies the temporary

HIGH TIDE

You haunt my mind
I plague your soul
But the depth of your love
Is all I want to know

You keep nothing hidden
Except how you feel
Will I ever know
If these waves are real?

I can't tell where we're at
All I know is: it's wet
Are we deep in the ocean
Or awaiting regret?

GROWING PAINS

I've tried to forget
I've tried to let go
I swear I've moved on
Or is it for show?
One thing I've learned and didn't know
My love for you isn't fleeting
This love only grows

IT'S IN THE EYES

You can barely speak
Your figure seems weak
You're being a sneak
But I can see it in your eyes

Don't you realize
You're testing morality
That damn drug
Disconnects you from reality

All anxiety is calmed
By swallowing a white pill
How do you walk through life
When you can't feel the thrill?

You're acting
Unjustifiably stormy
Can you please stop taking that prescription
For me?

You haven't stopped; I can see it in your eyes.

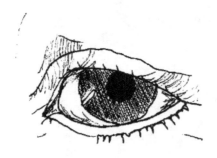

UP AND OVER

I miss his warmth
When it's cold at night
I miss his kind words
When I don't feel all right
I miss disappearing
Then waiting to be found
I miss laughing together
With no one around
I miss the fun
We had way back when
Despite all these things
I still don't miss him.

THIEF

Why am I still awake thinking about you?
First my heart, now my sleep
Why did I leave myself unlocked?
You're a sneaky little thief!

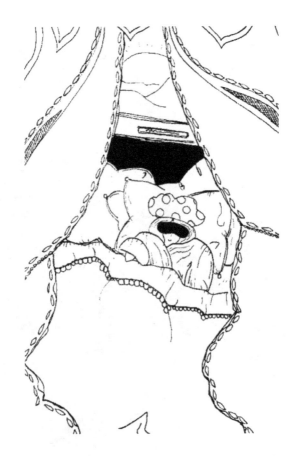

CHILDREN

I'm upset
You're annoyed
We ignore it
We're both so damn immature

I'm awake
You're asleep
We're both not OK
What happened to our fervor?

I'm not enough
You're too much
We're acting childish
You don't understand how I operate

I avoid
You sulk
We mentally hurt
Yet we still avoid setting things straight

I HATE YOU IF YOU KNOW

I don't know where I'm heading
I don't know where I'll land
I look around and feel
Like the only one without a plan

He's got two job offers
She's already in grad school
My future is undetermined
Does that make me a fool?

SUNDAY

The sky is gray
The cold wind bites
I love this day
But dread its night
A day of rest
For love, for some
I wish that Monday
Would never come

UNTIL THEN

I'm not independently sprouted
I know I'm not quite fully grown
I'll probably love you forever
But need another year alone …

AT LEAST!

BLOOM

Every moment we spend together,
I find myself wanting you more and more.
How will I be able to survive without you
In the year that follows?
Do you feel the same?
This vulnerability
Makes me want to push you away
And pull you closer
At the same time.
I keep telling myself …
Heartbreak is beautiful.
Heartbreak is inevitable.
It will come.
And I will grow.

THAT WOULD MAKE SENSE

There's a feeling in my stomach
I don't know what it's from
Not hunger
Not gas
Not a hangover
I just feel kind of numb

Lately I've been apprehensive
My emotions are all so crazy
I'm upset
I'm lonely
I'm angry
Sometimes I just feel hazy

Wish I knew what was happening
Maybe I just need some rest
Could be a cold
Could be stress
Could be seasonal
But maybe I'm just depressed.

IT STILL HURTS

We're going different ways
We don't work well apart
But if our paths ever cross again
You're the one who gets my heart

RADIO SILENCE

I wanted to talk
You wanted to sleep
I'll hold my breath
So you won't hear me weep

I want you to understand
You want my feelings to be done
Why care what I feel inside?
As long as I'm fun

This temporary love
Will be over next fall
I suffer in silence
You do nothing at all

FACT OF LIFE

|

People are assholes. People never stop being assholes.

POP

I feel like a water balloon
Continually filling with sorrow
Every inch of pain
Makes my latex exterior grow wider.

This pain I'm mentally inflicting
Has no meaningful cause
I get caught up in past problems
I long for what once was.

God forbid anything sharp
The slightest issue will make me feel worse
I don't know how much I can hold
Before this water balloon bursts.

"Ikey died."

POP

IKEY DIED

"Ikey died,"
Dad told me,
The pain running down his face.

We sat there,
And we wept,
Hoping for a sign from grace.

Carter came
The next day.
We held each other and cried.

How can we
Go on when
Our family glue has died?

TYPES OF PEOPLE YOU SEE AFTER A DEATH IN THE FAMILY

- The crier (best seller)

- The strong supporter (back rubs included)

- The person who brings food they made

- The person who brings food they bought

- The ones who offer sleeping pills

- The ones who bring wine

- The ones who drink way too much wine

- The random mourner (who are you again?)

- Necessary extended family

- Not-so-necessary extended family

- The good friends who hold you in their arms

- The ones who clean everything

- The people who send their love via the post

- The ones who stay with you even when you assure them that you're OK (gold stars for them)

MY ROCK IS GONE

I'm confused and shocked
How could you be gone?
You were my one true rock
How can I go on?

I'm hopelessly broken
My heart ripped into shreds
So many kind words spoken
But after them, you're still dead

I'm lost and unsure
Thinking you won't be there
To witness me mature
I need you; it's not fair

I'm trying to find peace
Doing the things that you would
But the pain won't cease
I don't think it ever could

I try to remember
You're physically gone, spiritually not
But I still miss you every day
You'll always be my rock.

NO MORE YOU

No more midday phone calls
No more funny texts
No more inspiring mentorship
No more opinions on what happens next

No more editing my papers
No more judgment on my clothes
No more trivia battles
No more scrapbooks to compose

No more snaggle-tooth smile
No more booming laugh in my ears
No more favorite face in a crowd
No more resting place for my fears

No more philosophical conversations
No more letters, comics, or jokes
No more hugs and no more high-fives
No more burgers for you to poke

No more freshly shaved head to touch
No more matching hands to admire
No more early-morning fitness
No more dreams for you to aspire

No more graphic T-shirts
No more crazy socks
No more see-you-tomorrows
No more "I love you. You're my rock"

No more of my advocate
In your place, there's now a hole
No more of all this
Because no more brother to fill the role.

SEE YOU SOON

I never thought that I
Would say goodbye so soon
We still had so much to conquer
We had so much left to do

When I lost you, I lost so many things
An enormous piece of my heart
My big brother, my teacher, my best friend
My one true counterpart

I often remember that Friday
Our final time together
Sipped tea, talked about life
Then you took off for your next adventure

We chose not to say goodbye
I pray our parting words prove true
Since we didn't say goodbye that final time
I really hope I see you soon

QUESTIONS THAT WILL
NEVER BE ANSWERED

Did you know you were dying?
Both when it happened and before.
Did you have a feeling?
Why couldn't it have been anybody but you?
It was supposed to be anyone but you.
Is heaven real?
Have you met our grandparents?
Are Jake and Bear there?
What happened as soon as you died?
Did everything go black? This thought induces anxiety.
Is there anything you wish you had done before?
Did you get to see everything we did for you?
Is there anything you want me to know?
Can you see me now?
Are you still you somewhere?
Please be you, somewhere.

YESTERDAY

I remember you in childhood
Mischief your favorite hobby
Causing trouble whenever you could
Larger than life, in mind and body

Your loved ones shared their stories
Which made us happy, yet upset
We love you more than you can imagine
So easy to remember, impossible to forget

All this love, nowhere for it to go
Beatles music is so fitting
The memories of the life gone
Seem more alive than the living

NORMALITY IS EVER-CHANGING

I'm forgetting to eat
I'm awake all the time
I've worn the same clothes for days
My lack of bathing is a crime

It's hard to leave my room
I spend every evening in tears
Random people keep sending condolences
This chick? We haven't spoken in years

I mainly feel I'm depressed
I have no true motivation
My friends don't understand
I empathize with their frustration

People tell me I'm "so strong"
But the breakdowns they don't see
I often feel utterly alone
Even with love surrounding me

Randomly, I'm grateful
What I lost, few ever get
I know this pain will pass
But I can't see the ending quite yet

Life is so tumultuous
Breaks in the agony prove brief
How the hell will I get through this?
Can one ever conquer grief?

THANKS?

I'm a lot more lonely
A little more blue
A lot more anxious
With attacks, that's new

Shock, grief, depression
I was already going through
But then you betrayed my trust
Finding reassurance in someone new

I was in a million pieces
You saw; you knew
But now I'm completely shattered
All thanks to you

WHAT'S SHE LIKE
WITHOUT ME?

In the near and far future,
you are going to think of me
and wish you were a part of my life.
You're going to see certain things
and wish you could share them with me.
You're going to wish you knew
what I was up to
and who I was with.
And I'll think of you
every now and then too—
always with a bit of disgust and pity.

DUST HAS SETTLED

People have stopped taking care of me.
No one comes to wake me up.
I've stopped receiving flowers.
The days are still so rough.

No more food is being made in my honor.
People keep me at a distance.
Your name goes unspoken.
I question my own existence.

I'm awake at dawn.
Memories make my heart crack.
The days keep coming,
Yet you're still gone.
I would do anything for you to come back.

PRINCESS AND THE WHAT?

I enjoy your laugh
I admire your hands
I'm soothed hearing you speak
Of your distant plans

You like my company
You LOVE your dog
If you're such a prince
Why aren't you a frog?

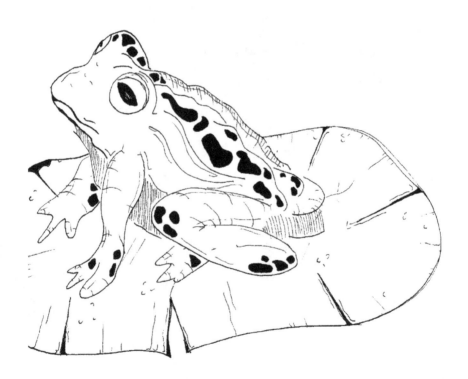

BERMUDA

Maybe I should be alone!
Perhaps, I should focus on me.
But I need a beach vacation …
And he tastes like the sea.

THE MORNING

Pulsing
Throbbing
Filling my head
Shaking my mind
With the words you said

Rattling around
Like a screw
In a box
On the hour
Strike musical clocks

Moving
And bouncing
And slipping away
The scenery fades
To a new day

YOU PROBLEM

He hurt me
While I was down
And left
When he saw
The effect
Of his actions

Then he came back
Just to blame me
For his own pain

But that
is no longer
My responsibility

The only obligation
I have now
Is to myself
And my own
Undistracted
Pursuit of happiness

SPRING-CLEANING

Spring has sprung!
And it's cleaning time.
Instead of the house--
I'm cleaning my mind

Threw out the
Worry
Jealousy
Envy
What's next?

Boxed up the
Judgment
Overthinking
Regret
Stress

Donated the
Fear
Anger
Shame
Shit I've kept since childhood

I used the
Self-loathing
Guilt
Resentment
As repurposed firewood

Out with these things
That have plagued my psyche
It's so nice in here now!
I really quite like it.

FACT OF LIFE

II

There are good people, and there are assholes, everywhere.

WHAT IS MY CRIME?

It's a deep,
Excruciating
Anguish.
I'm punched in the stomach
And ache all down my core.
My legs give out,
And I am forced to the floor.
I can feel the oppressor enter,
And I know what is coming.
Yet I am powerless
At keeping the pain at bay.
I'm struck in the chest
And hold my heart
As I gasp for air.
I'm choked,
And breathing becomes
Something I have to
Remind myself to do.
My vision gets blurry,
And all I can see
Are memories
Of a life that's gone.
I want to scream.
I do scream.
Yet
No one can hear me.
No one comes to my rescue.
My whole body shakes,
And I hold myself
Because no one
Is here to do it for me.
Missing you is
A form of
Cruel and unusual
Punishment.

NOT QUITE WHOLE

You toss out empty notepads
You don't use cups with cracks
There is no point for pointless pencils
Or chairs without a back

A puzzle that's missing pieces
Is not one that you attempt
Trying to use an empty pen
Only brings contempt

No one wants partial things
Complete—that's the goal
That's why I can't love you now
My heart isn't quite whole

LETTER WITHOUT A RESPONSE

You sat over me
And played "Stairway to Heaven"
Like my company wasn't new
I loved you for it
But I never told you.

I fell for you
Lying in your bed
Watching you play guitar
Shirtless and covered in me
The outside world felt so far.

We fell quickly
Into each other
And left few things unsaid
But I knew our days were numbered
As love grew, so did dread.

You wanted me
I wanted myself too
New life chapter; I began to depart
You wanted to remain in the pages
But I saw you as a bookmark.

I know you got my letter
And for one reason or another
You didn't reply
I know you think I'm a liar
But my feelings for you weren't a lie.

You were a light
At the very end
Of a long, dark tunnel
I wish the way we ended
Could have been a bit more subtle.

I'll always wish you well
I hope you find happiness in the new
You were worth the pain of losing another
You were worth the inevitable pain
Of leaving you.

THANK YOU, ADIEU!

You were not my first love
But the strongest flame
The burn carved a new person
Who grew through the pain

You'll be in the stills
But not in the moving
I'll keep the memories
While present pursuing

I left you behind
When I moved from Fife
You'll be in my heart
But not in my life

Your impact was large
Though your body is small
Your past was mine
Now we don't speak at all

MESSAGE DELIVERED

I hope you miss me sometimes.
I hope you get
little fits of nostalgia
and become lost
in memories of me.
I hope certain things
can bring you back
to the times we shared.
I hope you meet these memories
with gratitude
and sit with them
for a moment.
I hope you appreciate
the memories of me
before letting them
slowly drift away
as you focus
on your present.

OH, THAT OLD THING?

It's been months
Since I've gone a day without thinking about you
But in a way I didn't think before
I no longer crave your attention
I don't pester you when I'm bored

I don't hear a song and think of you
I don't send memes your way
I'm not dying to get your opinion
I'm not sad you're so far away

The memories are mine
And I appreciate all you taught
But I'm madly in love with my present now
What a wonderful thought!

HEARTBREAK LESSON

In the end,
I realized I'd held on for so long
because feeling loved
was more important
than the destruction
our relationship was causing.
I just wanted to know
someone cared.
From him,
I was reminded every day.
The emotions,
the highs and lows,
were flags of interest
that confirmed my place
in his heart.
In the end,
feeling loved wasn't enough
to last forever.
But it was enough
for a while,
and I'm a better person
for being on the other side.

FACT OF LIFE

|||

If it's making you feel like shit,
it's not meant to be.

TRY ME

Hit me, universe.
Give me your worst.
I can handle it now.

ST. ANDREWS

Out of town
Is three streets down
We party in black tie
Pier walks in red gowns

An unusual melting pot
In a small fishing village
Everyone's got a different passport
I'll marry you for a British

Small-town life can suffocate
Proximity is a privilege
But any issue you have
Becomes everyone's business

You can't do anything alone
Half the town has seen you nude
Frivolous matters get amplified
Drama gains excess magnitude

Though everyone complains
"This town can be so lame"
The distance now fills me with sorrow
I can no longer say "See you tomorrow"
To my favorite misfits
And mean it

OLD CHARACTER REVISITED

Our love was a lifetime ago
Though you've solidly remained the same
I feel I'm a new person
New mindset, different game

You knew me as a wild adolescent
During my most tumultuous youth
When we'd stay out late, sneak around
Never telling our parents the truth

We'd smoke and eat so much takeout
That we'd both feel deeply sick
We'd make love wherever we wanted
"This isn't safe. Make it quick"

We grew up and went separate ways
You crossed the Metroplex; I crossed the ocean
But now you live a ten-minute walk
From my new home on Goshen

The world suddenly stopped spinning
And I found myself content in your comfort
But as things slowly start moving again
I feel our days together are numbered

Here's the issue
You love every woman you see
On the phone, on the street, on the TV
I find no love left for me

The old me would have accepted the bits
Of love that you so graciously provide
But I left that girl in the past
Destruction of self when my brother died

I learned it's a waste to give yourself halfway
Real love doesn't come in parts
I think you're too irresponsible
To have my newly furnished heart

TO THE TRASH

Going back to an ex
Is like reheating old food.
Some people do so without a second thought.
Me?
I don't like leftovers.

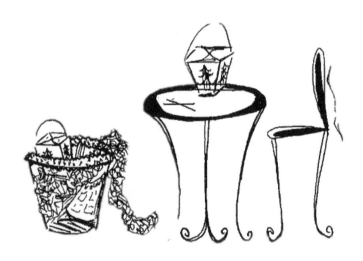

FACT OF LIFE

IV

Not everyone is made for white picket fences and early nights in.
Thank God.

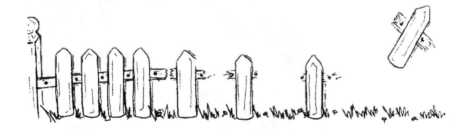

WITHOUT YOU

My favorite person doesn't exist anymore
I can't get it through my head
How does one ever come to accept
That your hero
Is dead

No matter how badly I want it to stop
Life keeps on keeping on
Though I feel time disappear
When I remember
Ike's gone

It's been a year, and I'm still in pieces
My new reality can get grim
One second, I'm OK
The next, I'm not
How do I be me without him?

GUTTER

Goddamn, this is hard
My confidence has changed
I fail every attempt
I can't stay in my lane

I give life a toss
All I want is a strike
But the safety net is gone
Where the fuck are you, Ike?

It's so hard to keep going
There's no view from the gutter
Life without my brother
Is like bowling without bumpers

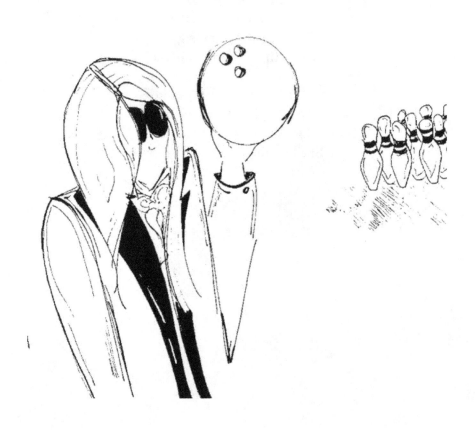

SPARKMAN

Your home was once an apartment
One with bunk beds and that ugly rug
I used to be greeted with laughter
Crooked smile, warm hug

It used to be a joyful car ride
Music blasting, happy passenger
I'd drive recklessly all the way
Must get to Ike—faster, FASTER

Reunion meant incoming judgment
"Cams, your clothes are so bizarre"
We'd exchange full life updates
Then we'd sing and play guitar

I used to come with friends
Now I prefer to come alone
Our banter is now one-sided
The only brother is written in stone

You still have frequent visitors
Though you're just a plate in the grass
When your buddies come, it's still a party
They bring you your own shot glass

You're still the first person I visit
When I arrive back to town
You're not at Dad's, not at your apartment
You're nestled softly in the ground

I speak out loud and cry shamelessly
Your neighbor's families try not to stare
The new grass that's grown above you
Is already longer than your hair

THE HEART

I sense you in the sun
I absorb you in the rain
I picture you in the ocean
I can feel you in my pain

As I sit at your grave
I just have to say
I'm so lucky I had you
But I wish you could have stayed

I wish you stayed
For the graduations
The weddings
The inevitable future deaths

I wish you stayed
To tell me you love me
No matter what life
Throws me next

You were the first gift I received
And the first real shatter to my heart
My only solace is in writing
This heartache fuels my art

I'LL TAKE YOU, GRIEF MONSTER

My new favorite antagonist
Can be quite the arrogant asshole
He loves putting me through pain
And making daily life a hassle

I can feel his shadow when he's coming
And he always arrives with a smile
I quickly lock my door
Aware we'll need privacy for a while

On days when I need to be happy
The grief monster lets me turn him away
Though he always returns at some point
Plans never canceled, just delayed

He plays painful memories in my head
And likes to see me in tears
He watches me scream out in agony
With an evil smirk—"Cheers!"

Grief monster reminds me what he's replaced
And although his presence proves upsetting
I choose his heart-wrenching company
Over the emptiness of forgetting

LIFE HACK

The trick to moving on
Is not to forget the past
But to embrace the present
So passionately
That you hardly look back

I ONLY NEED ME

If I commit,
I want someone
Who can love
The mess that I am.
Someone who will find beauty
In my faults
And make me feel loved
When I'm in the strangest states of mind.
I will not give my heart away
To someone
Anytime soon.
When I do,
It will only be because
I have found someone
Who adds as much value
To my life
As I add to theirs,
Which is a lot.

ALL OR NOTHING

I won't settle.
I won't assume someone will work out
And be my life partner for the original plot—
Get married!
Have kids!
And get boring!
No.
I want passion.
I want someone
Who feels like a drug.
I want someone
Who crosses my mind
Through the most mundane
Parts of my day.
I want someone
I want to be with because
I'm not only
Intensely infatuated with them
But also
So comfortable
That I can be my
Vulgar,
Dirty,
Emotional self.
I won't get married
To choose a husband.
I will marry a soul mate
Who wants me
And not a role
Or a place filler.
I'll marry

For heavy,
Intoxicating,
True love.
Not a day before.

Even then,
I won't change my name.

Write it in stone.

JOSEPH AND THE AMAZING TECHNICOLOR DREAMCOAT!

If you stitched my life into a blanket
Woven with every bit of my past
There'd be rainbow colors present
Though I often feel typecast

People tell me I radiate yellow
They assume life's been a breeze
But the smile sewn on my face
Doesn't indicate constant ease

I'd have green thread stitched throughout
For all the illnesses I've survived
Some physical, some mental, some not mine
But I made it; I'm alive

There'd be strong threads of indigo
Representing a life of drama
Those moments of pure melancholy
That reveal all past trauma

Violet string would show constant confusion
Those growing pains, you know?
I constantly have to push myself
To redefine *comfort zone*

All throughout the blanket
Would be the most beautiful red thread
Representing everyone I've loved and lost
Some I outgrew; some are dead

Orange would be quite obvious
Showing my drive and determination
I'd be throwing a pity party in Texas
Without courageous participation

On the outside, I am yellow
But that's the color I choose to show
Just like everyone, my colors go hidden
To appease those scared by rainbow

We all have diverse colors
We've all been dark blue
Some come in bright exteriors
But you don't know their true hue

If you stitched my life into a blanket
Multicolor threads would all be there
I'm done hiding my rainbow colors
Fuck it. Let 'em stare.

IKE'S LINES I MADE MINE

I don't know whether
To laugh or cry
Sink or fly
Or move on
I focus on what's mine
But the possessions intertwine
I don't know whether
To stay or go
Jump high or low
Shrink or grow
Or move on
I spin with the time
But never fast enough
To feel sublime
I don't know whether
To scream or shout
Go in or out
Use mustard or sauerkraut
Or move on
If I let myself go
I'll fall apart
But I'm wound so tight
Compressing my heart
I try to let myself
Simply be
But always find myself
On an extremity
Too tight or too loose
I never feel fine
I need some guidance
From the divine
Or maybe a body

To hold me in place
And keep my mind
Out of outer space
I feel like I'm crazy
And lazy
And strange
I need to move
To groove
And rearrange
I'm stuck in a box
That has no sides
But shrinks and grows
Just like the tides
I know it's there
They told me in school
Is this all just a game
To entertain some fool?
Watching and laughing
And drinking his tea
At the crazy people
Like you and me
Maybe we're all
On some big boat
Flooding the rapids
Of a galactic moat
Never getting closer
To the place we desire
Equidistance away
Until the day we retire
Disperse and go
In a million directions
To find a million
Different perfections
Face your fears and disappear
And come back strong
With the golden spear

All these ramblings
What the fuck?
I stole them from his book
That schmuck
I looked for answers
In the stolen possessions
The dead still here
Giving me new lessons
I needed to write
The drive wouldn't cease
So I stole this poem
From the journal
Of the deceased
I feel like a thief
But also relief
Maybe the deceased
Left this for me

THESE VERSES

Writing is the only form of therapy
That I've found to effectively calm my mind.
I find solace in solitude
And leave hardships and heartache behind.
Out of my heart, onto the page.
I write it in verse,
Then I'm done.
Until I have to go back and edit …

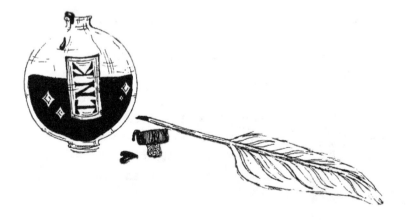

IF IT DON'T FIT, DON'T FORCE IT

I have all these old possessions
Cardboard boxes filled with tokens of life
They're large, stuffed, and sealed
They can't be opened with a knife

I've met a few familiar strangers
Who wanted me to use their storage
But I couldn't find the right space
Not one worth the mortgage

One stranger had copious room
And wanted me to fully use it
He had no boxes of his own
His cleanliness scared me, I admit

One ushered me in with enthusiasm
But had too many boxes of her own
I lost some of myself in her mess
The overstuffed place didn't allow growth

One tried to open my possessions
And wasn't at all gentle
He didn't realize my stuff was valuable
Not in cost; I'm sentimental

Then came along an old friend
Always there, never overbearing
She ushered me in with love
And the baggage we began sharing

My items filled her open space
Effortlessly, hers complemented mine
Soon a house became our home
All our boxes, one beautiful shrine

For her forks, I had the spoons
The knives we acquired together
She had so much summer clothing
I prepared us for cold weather

If it don't fit, don't force it
Don't stay where you can't unpack
Increasing your boxes or sizing them down
Don't do it! It's a trap!

AND THE PRINCESS

One morning, it just happened.
The war in her mind had come to an end.
Left in disarray, marked by destruction,
The damage she began to amend.

Happiness had been taken from her,
Monsters in her mind committing the theft.
Using her strength, she went to battle,
And now she'd won; the enemy left.

The struggle with a mental opponent
Required resilience and intellect to take down.
But what the darkness didn't know,
Its foe proved a princess
Who'd simply misplaced her crown.

The champion turned the heavy page,
Ending both dark days and that life's chapter.
This princess was now off
To find her happily ever after.

LIFE IS

Life is
a never-ending oscillation
between the incredibly wonderful
and the painfully awful.
You fight off the first round of monsters,
bask in the glory of their defeat,
then another comes straight at you.
You have to keep going.
You have to keep growing
in order to fight whatever comes next.
The hardships of the battles you face
are always worth the joy of the victory.

FACT OF LIFE

V

No matter what it takes, I will have a beautiful
life that I will enjoy and be proud of.

to be continued...

CPSIA information can be obtained
at www.ICGtesting.com
Printed in the USA
BVHW030507121220
595555BV00001B/25